Gervase Phinn's Yorkshire

Gervase Phinn's Yorkshire

A PICTORIAL JOURNEY

First published in Great Britain 2003 by
Dalesman Publishing Company Limited
Stable Courtyard
Broughton Hall
Skipton
North Yorkshire
BD23 3AZ
www.dalesman.co.uk

Text © Gervase Phinn 2003
Photographs © Dorothy Burrows, Chris Craggs, John Critchley/English Heritage, Alan Curtis,
Mike Kipling, John Morrison, Colin Raw, Roger Redfern, Bob Skingle/English Heritage, David Tarn,
Yorkshire Sculpture Park/Jonty Wilde 2003

A British Library Cataloguing-in-Publication record is available for this book.

ISBN 1 85568 207 9

Designed by Jonathan Newdick
Colour origination by Grasmere Digital Imaging Limited
Printed by Oriental Press, Dubai

Frontispiece: drystone wall by David Tarn.

CONTENTS

Introduction

The silhouette of Scarborough Castle from across the bay. The castle occupies a dramatic location on a sixteen-acre (6.5 ha) headland overlooking the town and the North and South bays. The site has been an attractive one from prehistoric times. It was utilised by Bronze Age peoples and the Romans, and was the site of an Anglo-Saxon monastery. The first castle was erected in c1135 by the Norman nobleman William le Gros, earl of Albermarle.

My parents were typical of many Yorkshire folk: industrious, good-humoured, generous and plain-speaking with strong views and a wry sense of humour. You would expect my parents to have a wry sense of humour, calling a child, born in a small redbrick semi in Rotherham, Gervase.

My father, a steelworker in the great foundry of Steel, Peach & Tozer in the dark and dirty Don Valley, was a great storyteller. I would sit on his knee, arms around his neck, and hear tales of pirates, ghosts and daredevil heroes. He was wonderful at accents and a master of dramatic timing, and I would listen enthralled. My mother, a nurse, read to me every night. As a small child I would take the words I had to learn home from school in a little round tin, and she would arrange them on the carpet and make up stories around them. Then she would read to me: *Peter Rabbit*, the works of Lewis Carroll, the parables of Jesus, Enid Blyton, 'The Selfish Giant' by Oscar Wilde, *The Water-Babies*, *The Wind in the Willows*, the stories of Hans Christian Andersen and *Tales from The Brothers Grimm*. I swam in a pool of language.

Then there were the outings. My parents were great day-trippers and most weekends found us — mum and dad, my two brothers, sister and myself — in a great green Morris Oxford heading for the coast. It was always the seaside. Mum would pack the boxes of sandwiches and fruit cake and fill the flasks, dad would check the car — tyres, oil, water — and we children would be waiting excitedly on the back seat, keen to be away. We left the smoke and grime of Rotherham behind us, and headed for Driffield and Market Weighton. It was usually my brother, Alex, who would ask first: 'Are we nearly there yet?'

If it was Bridlington, our first stop was the ice-cream parlour on the front, where dad would treat us to a 'knickerbocker glory'; that tall cone-shaped glass full of raspberry jelly, strawberries, chunks of tinned peach and different-flavoured ice-creams, scattered liberally with crushed nuts and topped with a shiny glazed cherry. Then followed a trip around the bay in the *Bridlington Belle*. If it was Filey, it would be a walk along the Brigg and have fish and chips on the harbour wall. Sometimes we would go further afield: to Staithes, where time seemed to have stopped; Sandsend and its great stretch of clean beach; Robin Hoods Bay, where we would explore the narrow entries and snickets;

Characterised by the stepped formation of its houses, which rise up the steep sides of the Calder Valley, is Hebden Bridge. In his *Journal*, John Wesley describes this flash of beauty, set deep in the industrialised valley of the Pennines: 'One can hardly conceive anything more delightful than the vale from which we rode from thence.'

and, of course, Whitby, with its quaint streets, picturesque quay and imposing abbey. One memorable Sunday my parents insisted we visit St Mary's Church in Whitby, situated high on the cliff top. We were told there was a magnificent view over the harbour from the church, and we could view the famous box pews and three-decker pulpit. One hundred and ninety-nine steps later, we arrived at the church but were not overly interested in the view or the famous box pews and three-decker pulpit. We were too tired. On the way home we children fell fast asleep on the back seat of the car.

Each summer we had a week at Scarborough in Mrs Hesketh's boarding house. I remember one holiday, we stood outside the entrance

of the palatial Grand Hotel. We marvelled at the Gothic splendour: cast-iron balconies, corner domes with porthole windows, the red and orange terracotta, and the great Corinthian columns. 'When I win the football pools,' Dad had said, 'we'll stay here.'

In the holidays I would explore with my school friends the area around Rotherham. In *A Six Month Tour Through the North of England*, Arthur Young, writing in 1770, described the route from Rotherham to Sheffield as 'execrably bad, very stony and excessively full of holes'. Clearly things had changed little, and on a bike ride out to Canklow Woods, I hit a pothole and ended up in Rotherham Doncaster Gate Hospital with a broken arm.

One favourite destination was Roche Abbey. We would cycle out to Wickersley, famous for the grindstones used in the Sheffield cutlery trade, through the mining town of Maltby and into the country, eventually arriving at the crumbling remains of the magnificent Cistercian abbey. Only the east end of the church remained, but one could sense by the outline of the stones how huge and imposing this building must have been. I returned recently on a cold winter's morning, when there was a light dusting of snow on the ancient stones. There was no sound or movement, and I was at once aware of the spirituality and tranquillity of this awesome place.

Another popular trip out was to the towering Norman fortress of Conisbrough Castle with its great circular keep and mighty buttresses. When I was a boy, Conisbrough Castle was a deserted roofless shell, but I remember sitting on the grassy mound staring up at the towering edifice and imagining knights in glittering armour, gallant Crusaders, dark dungeons and great battles. Recently refurbished, the castle is now a major tourist and education centre.

Rotherham has an unfortunate image: a decaying steel town, dark and uninteresting, the butt of the comedians' jokes. Few realise that seventy-five per cent of the borough of Rotherham is actually rural, and there is much to see in the town itself and the surrounding area. In the town centre stands the fine fifteenth-century All Saints' Parish Church, built of red sandstone and with a soaring 180-foot (55 m) spire, which is one of the finest examples of Perpendicular architecture in Yorkshire. A walk away is the Bridge Chapel of Our Lady with its battlements, parapets and pinnacles, a rare survival of medieval times.

Most Sundays, when I was a boy, I was out and about on my bicycle: trips to Clifton Park and museum; Boston Castle; Cusworth Hall which now houses the Museum of South Yorkshire Life; Wentworth Woodhouse and the huge stately home of the earls Fitzwilliam; Elsecar Reservoir; Sprotborough Canal; Swinton Lock; Thorpe Salvin with the remains of a fine Elizabethan mansion and small church of St Peter's;

Some may consider this wind-power turbine, towering above Naylor Hill sandstone quarry near Haworth, ugly and intrusive but I find the structure, which provides renewable, environmentally friendly energy, strangely impressive and rather elegant.

and Tickhill with its duck pond, buttercross, magnificent Perpendicular church, St Leonard's Tudor hospital and the sad remnant of a once-fine Norman castle. These attractions remain, but there is so much more for the young person these days — all within easy travelling distance from Rotherham: the Earth Centre, Abbeydale Industrial Museum, Magna, Doncaster Dome and, of course, Meadowhall. Not too far away are the National Coal Mining Museum, the Yorkshire Sculpture Park, the Museum of Photography, Film & TV in Bradford, and, in Halifax, Eureka, the museum of childhood, an experience no-one should miss.

I discovered the North York Moors in the sixth form. This silent and bleak world with its great tracts of heather and bracken fascinated me. My geography master, an inspirational teacher called J A Taylor, organised many a field trip at weekends and during the school holidays. We would stay in youth hostels and explore the incredible landscape, visit great abbeys like Byland and Rievaulx, eat our sandwiches in the shadow of the lofty castles at Helmsley and Pickering, and sit in the sunshine outside the local inns in villages untouched by modern life.

One weekend in June we walked from deep within the North York Moors towards the coast at Ravenscar. The journey followed the old Viking route known as the Lyke Wake. Legend has it that the Vikings carried the 'lyke' or corpse across the forty boggy miles (64 km) to the sea, where the body was given up to the waves. With the coming of Christianity, the practice was continued, but it took on a deeper meaning and the walk came to symbolise the journey of the soul towards heaven. I had never seen such magnificent scenery in my life.

Beneath a shining blue sky there stretched a landscape of every conceivable colour: brilliant greens, swathes of red and yellow gorse which blazed like a bonfire, dark hedgerows speckled in pinks and whites, twisted black stumps, striding walls and the grey snake of a road curling upwards to the hills in the far distance. Light the colour of melted butter danced amongst the new leaves of early summer.

Just before I started college to train as a teacher, my parents retired to Flamborough. Mum and dad had always loved this part of Yorkshire and I spent many a glorious summer exploring that part of the coast. A favourite walk was along the cliff top from Flamborough Head, passing the chalk-built octagonal lighthouse, Beacon Hill and South Landing, before reaching the deep ravine of Danes Dyke.

I have always wanted to be a teacher. My sister Christine taught in Sheffield and was a great encouragement, and my parents were keen that I should make the most of the educational opportunities. I studied for my degree and Certificate in Education at Leeds and a whole new area of the great county opened up. There was, of course, the bright and busy city itself; a few miles away was Nostell Priory, the fine Palladian house designed by the young James Paine; the Moravian village of Fulneck, a single street terrace of Georgian houses, the longest in Britain of its period; the magnificent Harewood House; and Bramham Park with its beech hedges and avenues of trees. My girl-friend at the time was a flame-haired, green-eyed Irish girl, and many a romantic evening was spent at Kirkstall Abbey, walking hand-in-hand by the river. Although overlooked by row upon row of terraced housing, and sandwiched between a busy dual-carriageway and a railway line, the abbey was a haven of tranquillity. It was on one beautiful summer evening, as we sat amidst the ruins, that my flame-haired Irish beauty told me she had met someone else — a microbiology student from Rochdale — and was ending our relationship.

My teaching practice was at St Thomas-à-Becket Roman Catholic High School in Wakefield. The school was a stone's throw from Sandal Castle. The castle's moment of notoriety came with the Battle of Wakefield in 1460 when the Lancastrians overwhelmed the brave Yorkists, killing the duke of York, heir to the throne. It was the greatest victory of the Wars of the Roses. Some lunchtimes I would escape from the bustle and noise of the school and have my sandwiches amidst the ancient ruins.

I have always loved ruined castles and abbeys. William Gilpin expressed my feelings much better than I could, when he wrote in 1786:

'A ruin is a sacred thing. Rooted for ages in the soil; assimilated to it and become, as it were, a part of it. We consider it as a work of Nature, rather than of Art. Art cannot reach it.'

This photograph captures the very essence of Hardcastle Crags near Hebden Bridge — the fascinating wooded valley with deep rocky ravines, fast-flowing becks, secret paths and woodland rich in natural history.

I soon forgot my flame-haired, green-eyed Irish beauty when I met Christine, my future wife. She is a Yorkshire lass through and through, descended (on her mother's side) from old West Riding stock. Christine introduced me to the splendour of Saltaire, the model village created by the great Victorian philanthropist Sir Titus Salt to house the workers employed at his huge mill, There was a hospital, alms-houses, school, library, park and church — but no pubs.

Christine introduced me to many delights in West Yorkshire: the Brontë Parsonage at Haworth; Rombalds Moor, and the Cow and Calf; and the eerie East Riddlesden Hall with its wonderfully sinister history of ghosts and murders. A favourite day out was to the St Ives Estate with the packhorse bridge and Druids Altar; and, of course, there were the delights of Shipley Glen, the wooded ravine and moorland plateau, ideal for courting and a canal trip though the famous Five Rise Locks at Bingley.

All my teaching career was spent in Yorkshire — in Rotherham, Sheffield and Doncaster. I could not conceive of living and working anywhere else. I loved the forthright children and my shrewd, good-humoured and often comical colleagues. The first headteacher I worked for — the erudite and charismatic Dennis Morgan — had all the qualities often possessed by Yorkshire people: generous to a fault, hard-working but with a blunt nature and a fierce honesty.

To my surprise and delight, after fourteen years in the classroom, I was promoted to school inspector, which came with a car and a plush office in Harrogate. The memory of my first school visit as a school inspector in North Yorkshire will remain with me all my life. I had never seen countryside quite as exquisite. In my first book *The Other Side of the Dale* I described it thus :

'The small square schoolhouse was enclosed by low, craggy, almost white limestone walls. Behind lay an expanse of pale and dark greens, cropped close by lazy-looking sheep. Further off the cold, grey fells, thick bracken slopes and long belts of dark woodland stretched to distant heights capped in a blue mist. The colouring of the scene was unforgettable on such a day. I had driven to the school early, along twisting narrow roads, and through the open car window I could feel the warmth of the September sun and catch the tang of leaf and loam and wood smoke. I had passed ancient trees, tranquil rivers, towering fells, great shaggy hills, stark grey outcrops, seas of dusky heather and even the shell of a gaunt castle, and had been filled with a huge sense of awe.'

I still feel that huge sense of awe for 'God's Own Country'. Yorkshire is a county of infinite variety and, to my mind, the scenery is without doubt the most varied and stunning in the British Isles. The county might not embrace within its sprawling borders the vast magnificence of the Scottish Highlands or the towering grandeur of Snowdonia, but there is a particular beauty in each of its diverse landscapes. The great Yorkshire writer, Laurence Sterne, author of *Tristram Shandy*, wrote in his 'Letter to Eliza' of 1767:

'Yorkshire ... O, 'tis a delicious retreat both from its beauty and air of Solitude; and so sweetly does every thing about it invite your mind to rest from its Labours and be at peace with itself and the world.'

Yorkshire is indeed, a 'delicious retreat' but, of course, it is the proud, plain-speaking people who make this county so very special. I love the warmth of spirit, the kindness, the unflagging hospitality and courage of my fellow Yorkshiremen and women, their sharp humour and shrewd, down-to-earth insight into human nature. 'Never ask a man if he's from Yorkshire', goes the traditional saying. 'If he is, he'll tell you anyway. If he's not, you'll only embarrass him.'

1 *Castles and great houses*

On a commanding ridge overlooking the River Calder is Wakefield's greatest treasure, Sandal Castle. Begun by the second earl of Warenne in the twelfth century and 'one of the ruins Cromwell knocked about a bit', it was here, at the bloody Battle of Wakefield in December 1460, that Richard Plantagenet, duke of York, met his untimely end. It was this unfortunate duke of York who marched his men to the top of the hill, then marched them down again.

Yorkshire abounds with magnificent castles, reminders of medieval splendour and testimony to the exceptionally high quality of design and construction.

At Richmond, Scarborough, Middleham, Skipton, Helmsley and Bolton Castle, great curtain walls, giant buttresses, spectacular towers and turrets, elaborate archways, great vaulted halls, massive gatehouses and impossibly steep ramparts have withstood siege after siege, and we can still marvel at them.

Sadly, in industrial South and West Yorkshire, little is left of the great castles at Pontefract, Thorne, Mexborough, Tickhill and Sandal to remind us of their former size and glory, but the sites are still well worth a visit, for they remain fascinating and mysterious features of the landscape.

One castle — Conisbrough — still looms tall and proud over the small industrial town. This was the castle which featured in Sir Walter Scott's epic romance of Ivanhoe and the Lady Rowena. With one of the oldest circular keeps in England and built of remarkably well-preserved ashlar stone, Conisbrough is a most forbidding medieval fortress and worth a special visit.

Yorkshire abounds with great houses too, and in the heart of the industrial landscape they stand solid and proud: Temple Newsam, arguably the finest brick building ever erected in England; Harewood House, surely one of the most magnificent of Palladian mansions ever built; and Nostell Priory, housing the finest collection of Thomas Chippendale furniture in the country. To the west of Doncaster lies Cusworth Hall, a Grade 1 Georgian mansion, and its landscaped grounds and Museum of South Yorkshire Life.

But the gem for me is Brodsworth Hall. Not as gracious as Temple Newsam or as grand as Harewood House, it is a relatively modest Victorian mansion but, because most of the original decoration, fixtures, fittings and furnishings have remained intact in faded splendour, it offers the visitor an unparalleled insight into the past.

Tall pines, like sentinel giants, line the woodland path leading to Wentworth Castle, near Barnsley.

Built in the 1350s in the Decorated style, the Chantry Chapel of St Mary at Wakefield is thought by some to be the best of the four such examples of bridge chapels in England (I prefer the one at Rotherham myself). Chantry chapels were partly shrines and partly a means of collecting money for the upkeep of the bridge. This chantry was 'restored' by Sir George Gilbert Scott in 1847, who intended to repair the badly decayed west front, but he was persuaded by the mason to replace it with a replica and transport the entire medieval west façade to Kettlewell Hall, where it became part of the boathouse on the lake.

The imposing and secluded summer house, on the side of Delfer Wood at Cannon Hall near Barnsley, offered visitors to the great house a peaceful refuge. Acquired by Barnsley Council after the Second World War, Cannon Hall is now a museum and country park.

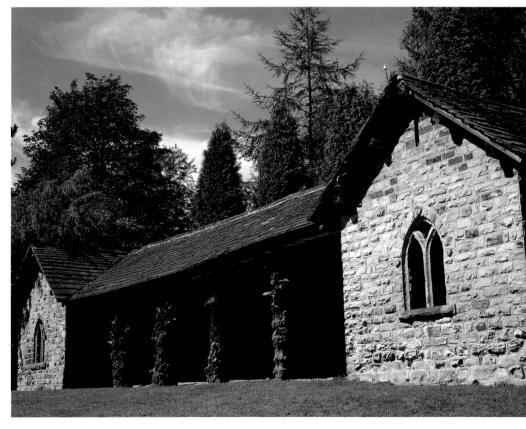

Left
'Twixt Leeds and Harrogate, and set in spectacular gardens, is Harewood House. Begun in 1759 by Edwin Lascelles, who made his fortune in West Indian sugar, this great treasure house of honey-coloured sandstone combined the talents of three great master craftsmen: John Carr, architect; Robert Adam, interior designer; and Capability Brown, who landscaped the park at a cost of over £6,000 — a staggering sum in those days.

GERVASE PHINN'S YORKSHIRE

Facing page, bottom
Dominating the landscape is the
forbidding fortress of Conisbrough
Castle near Doncaster, with its mighty
ninety-foot (27 m) tower and six
immense buttresses. Built in white
ashlar stone by Hamelin Plantagenet,
half-brother of Henry II, in the late
1180s, it rises majestically from a
mound overlooking the River Don.
This, the most impressive medieval
building in South Yorkshire, was
constructed to be impregnable.

Below
The magnificent Jacobean country
house of Temple Newsam near Leeds
is set in extensive parkland landscaped
by Capability Brown in the eighteenth
century. It was here that the weak and
violent Lord Darnley, second husband
of Mary, Queen of Scots was born.
The mansion, which was sold to Leeds
Corporation in 1922, houses one of the
finest collections of decorative art,
furniture, silver and porcelain in the
North of England.

The elaborate Italianate entrance hall of Brodsworth, with scagliola (imitation marble) columns and pilasters, ornate plaster ceilings, floors decorated with Minton tiles, and crimson Axminster carpets and hangings, has been conserved largely as it was found. The house has suffered from the ravages of damp, dust and woodworm, but reveals the wealthy Victorian's appetite for opulence and ornamentation. The original varnish has darkened with age, the paint has flaked and over-zealous cleaning has damaged the decorated marbling. English Heritage, which took over the estate in the 1990s, decided to preserve this fine example of a Victorian country house as it was.

Brodsworth Hall stands square and solid in its own extensive and secluded parkland, woodlands and shrubberies. Built and furnished between 1861 and 1863 by the banker Charles Sabine Augustus Thellusson, the house was designed by the architect and sculptor Chevaliere Casentini in the Italianate style and constructed in soft, pale, magnesian limestone. Over the years mining subsidence, water penetration and erosion have caused serious damage to the building and the gardens grew wild. Before opening the house and grounds to the public in 1995, English Heritage undertook careful restoration and conservation, and the result is quite remarkable.

2 *Museums and visitor attractions*

A £50 million Millennium initiative created the Earth Centre near Doncaster. Built into the hillside for extra insulation and with a huge solar canopy to provide enough energy for the site, much of the amazing structure is made from reclaimed materials. An ugly and disused pit and slag heap was transformed into an imaginative project for regeneration, renewable energy sources and environmentally friendly thinking.

It is all very well children reading about coal mining and steel working, how machines work and how we should cherish the environment, but the very best way for them to learn and understand is to appreciate it first hand. The museums now are not daunting, hushed places where exhibits gather dust in glass cases; they are active experiences.

Yorkshire has a wealth of museums which give an insight into the past. I only fully appreciated what a tremendously hot, dirty and physically demanding job my father did as a 'steelo' when I visited the magnificent Magna at Templeborough, situated midway between Sheffield and Rotherham. The Steel Experience, devoted to the heritage of steel-working, is a treasure house of memorabilia, archive photography and information, but the highlight is the working electric arc furnace, where sparks fly and metal melts before your eyes.

Situated to the east of Wakefield in a seventeen-acre (7 ha) rural setting, the National Coal Mining Museum paints a fascinating picture of the lives of coal miners through the ages. We visited in 1988, when the museum first opened, and my children were over-awed by the rather eerie and atmospheric underground tour when an experienced miner, and great raconteur, guided us through the underground workings.

Near Conisbrough is the Earth Centre, a four-hundred-acre (160 ha) park of beautiful gardens, fascinating exhibitions and attractions, and many outdoor activities, dedicated to encouraging the conservation and careful use of the world's resources.

At Eureka! The Museum for Children in Halifax there are six amazing environments to explore — town and country, jungle and ocean, ice and desert — to amaze and inspire children of all ages.

The new visitors' centre at the Yorkshire Sculpture Park, at Bretton Hall near Wakefield, is approached along a 330 foot (100 m) pathway made of square sheets of chequered plate steel with punched stencil-cut names. This 'Walk of Art', created by Gordon Young in celebration of the sculpture park's twenty-fifth anniversary, displays the names of those who have donated money to help maintain and improve the park.

Displayed throughout the 500 acres (200 ha) of eighteenth-century landscaped grounds which comprise the Yorkshire Sculpture Park are the most unusual and stunning modern and contemporary works by leading UK and international artists, such as this one, *Curved Reclining Form (Rosewall)*, 1960-2, by Barbara Hepworth. My son Matthew, who has a degree in fine art from Leeds University, was an invaluable guide when we last visited.

Barbara Hepworth said: 'I, the sculptor, am the landscape'. There are some spectacular landscapes at the Yorkshire Sculpture Park: sweeping views over the valley, copses ablaze with autumn's leafage, rolling verdant parkland and sheltering, full-leaved trees. Here a majestic cedar tree dwarfs her *River Form* (1965) and *Figure*.

The Nature Works building at the Earth Centre near Doncaster seems to float on one of the wildlife ponds. It looks unprepossessing, but this simple, lightweight structure, made of standard-size timber sections and simple joints, and designed by Matthew Letts, is unique. It houses specially constructed podiums which explore the land and water habitats at the centre.

One of the awesome exhibits at the National Coal Mining Museum resembles something from the set of a sci-fi film. The museum, which occupies a seventeen-acre (7 ha) rural site, has all the buildings found at a traditional colliery, and provides a fascinating insight into the lives of the miners through the ages and the machines they operated.

3 *Wild countryside*

This strange and craggy rock formation known as Bridestones, which stands incongruously on the moors above Todmorden, is a splendid example of a natural architectural feature which can be created by tens of thousands of years of erosion.

Sheffield is the highest city for its size in Europe, rising to 1,502 feet (458 m) in the west at High Nebb in Stanhope Edge. It is more closely surrounded by hills and steep ground than any other industrial city in Britain. To the west of the city is the Yorkshire Peak District, which must rank amongst England's loneliest and most desolate tracts of land — the nearest thing to wilderness in the Peak District National Park

The late John Hillaby, walker and naturalist, described the Dark Peak moors in his book *Journey Through Britain* as a 'land at the end of its tether. All life has been drained off or burnt out, leaving behind only the acid peat. You can find nothing like them anywhere in Europe.' The only sound he heard as he crossed the dark and lonely moors was the melancholy chirping of the meadow pipit, sounding to him like 'the last ticks of a clock that had almost run down'.

There are no ruined castles here, picturesque abbeys, quaint hamlets, frothing waterfalls or rich vegetation. It is bare and bleak, without tree or shrub. Yet the landscape of rolling moors, chocolate-brown 'hags' (banks) and 'groughs' (natural drainage channels) of peat which stretch for mile after mile, waves of dark heather and the occasional wind-blown farmstead, has a stark dignity.

Facing page
Waymarked walks lead into the valley
at Hardcastle Crag Woods and link
with the footpaths of the Pennine Way.
The walker, following the path through
dense woodland, will suddenly come
upon magnificent unspoilt greenery
and hidden waterfalls.

Dominating the skyline between
Hebden Bridge and Todmorden stands
Stoodley Pike, a 120 foot (37 m) high
stone obelisk which has acted as a
mecca for walkers for many years.
Local residents celebrated Napoleon's
exile to Elba in 1814 by raising funds
to build a tower. This first tower
collapsed in 1854 during a storm, and
a second one was built in 1856 which
has survived to this day.

Sheep graze safely on the treeless and
windswept moorland above Rishworth
in Calderdale. Such lonely splendour
looks too bleak and austere for man,
yet our Neolithic ancestors settled
here, for arrowheads, axes and other
artefacts have been discovered.

The lonely and deserted farmhouse at Crimsworth Dean, on the south-facing slope of the upper Hebden Valley, stands above open, treeless pastures.

The tranquil scene at Redcar Tarn, the nature reserve west of Keighley. This popular tourist attraction is a stone's throw from the attractive villages of Low Utley, Laycock and Braithwaite, and the famous Turkey Inn at Goose Eye, renowned for its real ale which is brewed on the premises.

The strong encircling arm of the River Calder meanders along the valley bottom. The name Calder, which comes from the Celtic meaning 'rocky or rapid-flowing water', seems inappropriate here. This great river, which rises in the South Pennines on Heald Moor at Todmorden and joins the River Aire at Castleford, fifty-six miles (90 km) from its source, flows for much of its length through the industrial towns of West Yorkshire. With the coming of the Industrial Revolution, the Calder powered textile mills by the score and became 'the hardest-worked river in England' — and one of the most polluted.

4 Mill towns

By the River Calder, in a beautiful well-wooded vale with high crags at a distance, is Hebden Bridge. Millstone grit terraced houses built on top of each other climb up the hillside. One memory of my visit to Hebden Bridge was when I spoke at the literary festival. The solid Victorian school, where the event took place, had a flight of extraordinarily steep steps leading up to the building which had been worn away over the years by countless scholars.

West Yorkshire is famous for its mill towns which flourished at the time of the Industrial Revolution. Plentiful supplies of water, rich and readily available coal deposits, and the development of steam power resulted in the rapid growth in the woollen and cotton industries.

Dewsbury did a roaring trade in shoddy (textiles made from reprocessed woollen cloth), Holmfirth was the centre of worsted cloth manufacture, Stanbury was famous for spun cotton and Heptonstall for hand-loom weaving. At Hebden Bridge, fustian cloth was a speciality and, at the huge mill at Saltaire, alpaca and mohair were produced.

The cloth industry has now declined but the mill towns have reinvented themselves, diversified, continued to flourish and have become attractive places to visit. Hebden Bridge, surrounded by dense woodland and having a range of interesting shops, a popular annual literary festival and a canal marina, is a thriving tourist centre. John Wesley, writing in his journal in 1757, speaks of this flash of beauty deep within the industrialised valley of the Pennines. 'There can hardly conceive anything more delightful', he wrote, 'than the vale from which we rode from thence.'

There is no market in Yorkshire to compare to Dewsbury's; over 400 stalls sell everything from tripe to toiletries, black pudding to lengths of cloth. Stanbury, a couple of miles (3 km) west of Haworth, and Heptonstall are two of the best-preserved hill villages in Yorkshire and are full of hidden treasures. In Heptonstall, the octagonal Methodist chapel perches high above Hardcastle Crags, and, in the graveyard by the Victorian church, the tombstone of the tortured poet, Sylvia Plath, stands incongruously between those of generations of Yorkshire folk. The great mill at Saltaire now houses the David Hockney exhibition and boasts an amazing range of shops. And, of course, Holmfirth got a new lease of life when it became the setting for the popular television series *Last of the Summer Wine*.

Surrounding these towns are stunning landscapes: deep valleys, huge tracts of moorland, reservoirs and rivers, windswept uplands and verdant lowlands, which make it wonderful walking country.

The view over Marsden shows the huge mill in the valley bottom, solid and imposing, and surrounded by rich pastureland and rising fells. It was in this mill that the Luddites destroyed the machines in a futile attempt to stop the new methods of production. Nearby is the tomb of Enoch Taylor, a blacksmith and Luddite leader.

GERVASE PHINN'S YORKSHIRE

A boundless view over Crimsworth Dean with its scattered farms and green sheltered softness, sweeping up to the rough moorland and bleak distant fells.

Yorkshire is full of quaint and curious customs. Arguably the world's oldest drama — traced back through English and European mummers' plays to Ancient Egypt and Syria — is the Pace Egg Play, enacted on Good Friday. The drama, performed here at Heptonstall, is a mixture of Pagan rebirth ceremony and Christianity folklore, and celebrates the triumph of good over evil.

Right
Four miles (6.5 km) west of Huddersfield in the picturesque Colne Valley is Slaithwaite, pronounced 'Slawit' by its inhabitants. The town grew rapidly in the Industrial Revolution when huge mills were built, harnessing the available water power. The Huddersfield Narrow Canal allowed goods to be shipped to the markets, and by the end of the nineteenth century Slaithwaite was a major textile centre with its own docks. The town is the setting for the television series *Where the Heart is*.

GERVASE PHINN'S YORKSHIRE

This magnificent building — the Piece Hall in Halifax — was saved from demolition by just one council vote. Opened by cloth merchants in 1779 for handloom weavers to sell their pieces of cloth, it was conceived as an Italian piazza — a public square or market place — enclosed by two or three storeys of colonnaded galleries housing over 300 small trading rooms. In 1928 the Piece Hall — the only surviving cloth hall in Yorkshire — became officially recognised as an ancient monument. Reopened in 1976, it now houses an art gallery, offices and shops, and featured in the film *Brassed Off*.

The mill dam at Luddenden Dean is a haven of peace and unspoilt greenery in a sea of industrialisation. Known as 'Little Switzerland', the name Luddenden derives from the Ludd Valley or 'valley of the loud stream', and as early as the thirteenth century a corn mill was established here.

The dramatic view over the thickly
wooded Hardcastle Crags and the
imposing hills beyond captures the
splendour of this unique area of
Yorkshire.

5 Industrial heritage

'Bradford for cash,
Halifax for dash,
Wakefield for pride and for poverty.
Huddersfield for show,
Sheffield, what's low,
Leeds for dirt and vulgarity.'

(From *English Folk Lore* by A R Wright, 1928)

During the Industrial Revolution, great tracts of pastoral South and West Yorkshire were blackened, ravaged and polluted. Fifty years ago in the industrial towns and cities, the air was full of soot and dust which turned town halls to immense grim monuments and houses to blackened rows. Farm lands disappeared, old towns and villages were transformed by mines and mills, and England's 'green and pleasant land' became dark and ugly.

As a boy, on my way to watch Sheffield United, I remember well the bus ride from Rotherham to Sheffield via Attercliffe. Down the Don Valley we went, end to end with filthy sheds, yards of scrap, rusty cranes, huge overhead transporters. It was an area which contained little but ugliness.

This grim image, however, was not the whole truth. A bus ride in the other direction took me to open country. Such beauty so close to heavy industry comes as a great surprise to visitors to the area. Over the last two decades the landscape has undergone a dramatic change. Heavy industry has declined, fish have returned to the once-polluted Don and, along its banks, willows grow and shrubs flourish.

In West Yorkshire, too, things have changed. With the decline of the woollen and worsted industry, some of the mills have been adapted for light industry and commercial use, and become listed buildings. Not all the mills were ugly monstrosities. Titus Salt created his vast T-shaped mill at Saltaire in Italianate style; Samuel Cunliffe-Lister, who built the 249-foot (76 m) high stack at Manningham, was keen to erect a building which was aesthetically pleasing; and, in Leeds, the Tower Works, built in 1864 to manufacture textile machinery, was based upon Lamberti's bell tower in Verona. Restored and cleaned, they are impressive and unusual buildings, not without architectural merit.

Opened on the 21st March 1774 to the sound of music, guns and cheering, the Five Rise Locks at Bingley are masterpieces of civil engineering, designed by John Longbotham of Halifax and constructed in ashlar millstone grit by local labour. Climbing steeply up to the watershed of the Pennines, here at Bingley the canal ascends by an extraordinary staircase of locks, high above the town, and, over a distance of 320 feet (100 m), boats are raised nearly 60 feet (18 m).

Yorkshire is nothing if not a county of great contrasts. What could be more different from the great shaggy hills and grey-green fells of the Dales or the barren windswept acres of the North York Moors than this scene of a tanker making its slow progress on the River Aire? The great cooling towers at Ferrybridge, 370 feet (115 m) high, can be seen towering in the distance. Ferrybridge, one the country's largest power stations, generates enough electricity to meet the needs of almost the entire population of West Yorkshire.

Beneath a vast cloudy sky, a petroleum
tanker moors at the Fleet Oil Depot
on the Aire and Calder Navigation.
Barges like the *Humber Energy* (pictured)
are up to 200 feet (60 m) long and 20
feet (6 m) wide, and discharge petrol
and oil at the wharves at Castleford
and Fleet.

Right
Sir Titus Salt (1803-76) created the model village of Saltaire for the workers at his vast mill in Shipley, opened in 1853. Having made a fortune in alpaca and mohair, he decided to move his operation away from the overcrowded and polluted town of Bradford into the country. Salt envisaged a community centred on the mill, with workers' housing of high quality, and with opportunities for education, recreation and health care. Over twenty years, 820 houses, in long terraces, were built in Yorkshire stone, to accommodate the 4,500 workers.

Facing page, bottom
The solid Gibson Mill, at Hebden Bridge in the tranquil Calder Valley, is hardly the 'dark and satanic' type of Blake's memorable poem or the massive Italianate edifice constructed by Sir Titus Salt at Shipley. Built in 1800, this former water-powered cotton mill is modest by comparison.

Below
On my visits to the Selby schools, I would pass Drax. The very name conjures up something strange and rather sinister. Yet this vast complex, Western Europe's largest coal-fired power station, is far from that. It is a spotlessly clean and modern facility. The sulphur emissions from the six huge boilers, which generate one tenth of Britain's total energy demand, are neutralised, thus reducing the effects of acid rain.

6 Haworth and Brontë country

The eerie and atmospheric scene at Haworth Church, where gravestones crowd in on each other. One could imagine Count Dracula here, emerging from behind a tombstone or the trunk of one of the skeletal trees. It is estimated that over 40,000 souls are buried in this graveyard, including Martha Brown, a servant of the Brontës, who died in January 1880. The Brontë sisters (except Anne, who is buried at Scarborough) are buried in the vault inside the church.

In 1857, Mrs Gaskell, in her biography of Charlotte Brontë, wrote of this bleak moorland town, which fired the imaginations of the three remarkable sisters:

'[The traveller] can see Haworth for two miles before he arrives, for it is situated on the side of a very pretty steep hill, with a background of dun and purple moors, rising and sweeping away yet higher than the Church, which is built at the very summit of the long narrow street. All round the horizon there are the same line of sinuous wave-like hills; the scoops into which they fall only revealing other hills beyond, of similar colour and shape, crowned with wild bleak moors. Right before the traveller, the road rises to Haworth.'

The surrounding countryside has changed very little since then, but the town itself is very different from how it must have been. Once Haworth was a squalid, industrial place, thick with black chimney smoke and the incessant noise of the chattering looms; a dark and desolate moorland blot on the landscape. Matthew Arnold, visiting the town in April 1885, wrote of the church as 'lonely and bleak', the colliers' carts 'poaching the deep ways' and the 'rough, grim'd race' who lived there. Haworth is now a lively, attractive place with comfortable tearooms, street theatre, antique and craft shops. The Brontë Parsonage Museum has a priceless collection of manuscripts, first editions and memorabilia.

My daughter Elizabeth, studying *Wuthering Heights* for A-level, prevailed on me to join her on the trek to Top Withens. This was a favourite spot for Emily Brontë and the inspiration for her great novel. It was an exhilarating experience.

Haworth is the headquarters of the Keighley and Worth Valley Railway, which serves six stations in the course of its five-mile (8 km) length. Originally built in 1837, the Worth Valley Railway has been restored, and a magnificent steam train trundles through the Worth Valley from Keighley to Oxenhope. There are picnic areas *en route* and, at the end of the line, a shop, buffet car and exhibition centre.

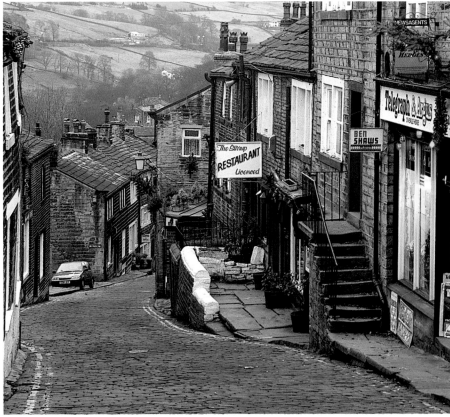

Left
The Parsonage at Haworth, now a museum and a shrine for all admirers of the three talented sisters, gives a fascinating insight into the isolated world of the Brontës. This plain Georgian house, dating from 1779, and surrounded by spreading trees and crowded tombs, has a melancholy dignity. It was the home of the Reverend Patrick Brontë, who was perpetual curate at Haworth from 1820 to 1861, and his family.

Above
Haworth, built in millstone grit like so many South Pennine villages, preserves its rugged character. From the top of the steep cobbled street one can see the scattered farms and woodland, and the great sweep of hill leading to the distant bleak moors.

As a result of the dedicated efforts of the railway enthusiasts who formed a preservation society, the Keighley and Worth Valley line, closed by British Rail in 1962, was saved and the stations like this one at Oakworth rescued from demolition. This magnificent and carefully-preserved Edwardian station, which has been winner many times of the Best Restored Station competition, featured in the film of the classic children's story *The Railway Children*.

Railway carriages at Oxenhope Station glisten in the rain. After the Second World War the passenger rail service was not restored and when the station finally closed in 1961, Oxenhope had just one siding, and was rather a sad and forlorn place. Today the station, with large free car park, buffet, shop and picnic area, is the base for operational coaches and has become a favourite tourist attraction.

The contrasting landscape of wild
moorland in the foreground and soft
green pastures in the background
could not be more striking in this
panoramic view from Penistone Hill
near Haworth to Sladen Bridge.

Facing page
This landscape, near Stanbury, is
Brontë country: a land of grey,
clustered homesteads and drystone
walls spreading like a mesh across
open fields, treeless pastures and small
copses, swelling contours and, rising
above all, the brooding moor. It was
from Stanbury that my daughter and
I walked up to Top Withens (reputedly
the setting for 'Wuthering Heights').

7 York

The mighty Minster, the largest medieval Gothic cathedral in Europe, soars above the rooftops at York. The poet Robert Southey was overwhelmed by its towering grace, although there is a sting in his adulation. 'The praise must be given', he wrote, 'to the English heretics that they preserve these monuments of magnificent piety with proper care.' Built on a site which has been in use for nearly 2,000 years, this treasure house of history and architecture has survived at least four fires since 1137, the last being in 1984 when lightning wrecked the south transept roof.

York: ancient port, garrison town, ecclesiastical and administrative capital of the North, is one of England's most beautiful and fascinating cities. One enters the city, enclosed by almost unbroken walls, through formidable medieval gateways to discover magnificent half-timbered buildings like St William's College, fine seventeenth-century brick houses such as the Dutch House, elegant Georgian residences and tranquil gardens, narrow streets, snickleways and cobbled yards, Roman columns, ancient towers and battle-scarred parapets — evidence of York's glorious past.

Towering above everything is the mighty Minster, the Metropolitan and Cathedral Church of St Peter, York's crowning glory, described by the poet Robert Southey as 'a monument of magnificent piety'. A very proud moment in my life was when, in 2002, an honorary fellowship of St John's College was conferred upon me in the Minster.

For almost 2,000 years York has been at the very centre of great historical events. Some of England's bloodiest battles were fought on the flat land around York: Stamford Bridge, when in September 1066 King Harold defeated his brother Tostig and the Norwegian king Harald Hardrada, in the prelude to the Battle of Hastings; Towton Moor, when in 1461, during the Wars of the Roses, 30,000 men died; and Marston Moor, when, during the Civil War, Prince Rupert's army was crushed and 3,000 Royalists were killed.

York is steeped in history, and has some of the finest and most imaginative museums in the country. These include the Archaeological Research Centre (ARC), a fascinating hands-on exploration of York's past; the National Railway Museum, a truly amazing exhibition covering 200 years of railway history; the innovative Jorvik Centre, where time cars transport you back to the era of the Vikings; the intriguing Museum of Automata; the Regimental Museum; Castle Museum; and the Yorkshire Museum which houses an extraordinary collection of Roman antiquities.

Some years ago I was asked to present prizes at St Olave's, the junior department of St Peter's School, reputedly the oldest school in England. The portrait in the great hall intrigued me. I knew the face so well. When I enquired of the Master as to whom it was, he informed me it was one of the old boys of the school: Guy Fawkes.

Below
In College Street, York (formerly Vicars' Lane), is the medieval black-and-white timbered façade of St William's College, named after a relative of William the Conqueror and who was archbishop of York in 1153. Originally it was the home of the priests serving the Minster but, after Henry VIII's suppression of monastic orders, the building passed into private hands. It is now the Cathedral Visitors' Centre. One famous owner was the ill-fated Charles I, who set up a press here to print leaflets or paper bullets, in a futile attempt to win the propaganda campaign of the Civil War.

Right
No visit to York would be complete without a visit to the fascinating Jorvik Centre and to join in the fun at the Jorvik Festival. Every February there is a re-enactment of a variety of Viking events, including the battle between the Danish King Sven's army and King Aethelred's. There are storytellers, entertainers and a Viking wedding, and the centre of the city is crammed with stalls set out like a Viking market and selling handmade traditional wares.

This view down the River Ouse captures the contrasting buildings in the great city of York. Most prominent is the Guildhall and its adjoining council buildings on the right. Built in the fifteenth century as a meeting place for the powerful merchant guilds (which effectively controlled government and business in the city), the Guildhall has a fascinating history. In one of the surviving chambers (committee room one), the Scots met the Roundheads and were paid in hard cash for the hand-over of Charles I who had taken refuge in Scotland after the Civil War. The money was carefully counted out on the table. In 1586, Margaret Clitherow was tried here for harbouring Catholic priests and sentenced to death by crushing. She was canonised in 1970.

This view of the Minster from the city walls shows the cathedral's size and beauty. The Venerable Bede wrote that the first church here was built in the seventh century. Since then there have been two Norman cathedrals, followed by the present building, completed at the end of the fifteenth century.

The imposing medieval gateway of Micklegate Bar has witnessed some of the bloodiest moments in the city's history. Built between the twelfth and the fourteenth centuries, it stands across the ancient route from London to York. Successive kings and queens have passed through here — not all as happy as Elizabeth II, who was welcomed through this gate in 1971. In 1461 the then duke of York had his head spiked here so that, as Queen Margaret says in Shakespeare's *Henry VI*, 'York may overlook the town of York'. Heads of the Jacobites captured in the 1745 Rising were also displayed here.

8 North Yorkshire coast

Flat rocks look like stepping stones stretching across the vast expanse of sand at Saltwick Bay, near Whitby. Almost directly east-west orientated — as such, the sun rises and sets in the sea for about a month every year around the midsummer solstice — this part of the East Coast has the most stunning sunsets.

Whitby, the burial site of the Celtic saints, is a special place to visit. Situated at the centre of the North Yorkshire and Cleveland Heritage Coast, Whitby's picturesque quaysides, spanned by a swing bridge, line both sides of the River Esk's wide mouth. This former whaling centre is where Captain Cook, arguably the world's greatest maritime explorer, learnt his trade. There are quaint streets to explore, steep-cut steps leading to narrow alleys and cobbled yards, the jet workshop and a superb museum to visit, the delightful Whitby Bookshop to browse around, Pannett Park in which to spend a peaceful hour and, according to our family, the best fish and chips in the country.

Whitby's skyline is dominated by the ruins of the thirteenth-century Benedictine abbey. Here in AD 657 came the formidable Abbess Hilda to establish a double monastery for monks and nuns. For the stout-hearted there is the 199-step climb to see the magnificent cliff-top parish church of St Mary, but avoid this on cold dark nights. Bram Stoker used the dramatic setting of the graveyard for a scene in his horror epic *Dracula*.

Five miles (8 km) south of Whitby is Robin Hoods Bay, a huddle of small red pantiled cottages and imposing eighteenth-century villas, haphazardly clinging to the steep cliff. Here, in the labyrinth of cobbled ginnels, interconnecting alleyways and steps, smugglers evaded the customs men and press-gangs waited to catch unwary victims. Robin Hoods Bay was the home of one of my favourite authors, Leo Walmsley, whose tales of treacherous tides, stormy seas and feuding fisher-folk, my father used to read to me as a child.

North of Whitby is a string of small villages — Runswick Bay, Hinderwell and Staithes — each with immense charm and fascinating histories. There are stunning sea views at Kettleness, where an entire village slipped into the sea in 1829, and at Port Mulgrave, once a busy port, which shipped out iron ore to the foundries at Jarrow. Nearby is Sandsend, with one of the finest sandy beaches in the region. My favourite time to visit Sandsend is in winter when I park the car on the roadside outside the village, wrap up well and walk the couple or so miles along the coast to Whitby with salt spray on my face and the huge crashing waves to my left.

Above
Nestled under the protective arms of the cliffs with wild moors behind, Staithes is a picturesque and unspoilt coastal town, 'singularly situated in a narrow creek between two cliffs and so near the shore that the sea reaches the houses at high water' (Rev John Graves in his *History of Cleveland*, 1808). Once an important fishing centre on the North Yorkshire coast, it was the town where the young James Cook started an apprenticeship in a haberdashers.

Right
The clutter of houses with their orange pantile roofs surround the mouth of the River Esk as it meets the North Sea here at Whitby. The old town, huddled under the steep western cliff, is a maze of narrow alleys and cobbled yards. On the cliff top is the Church of St Mary, adjacent to the ruined abbey of St Hilda.

NORTH YORKSHIRE COAST

Wheeling gulls fill the sky over Staithes.
Known locally as 'Steers', this is one of
the least spoilt coastal villages on the
North Yorkshire coastline.

Left
A charming jumble of whitewashed walls, grey slate roofs and orange pantiles lead down a cobbled walkway and almost into the sea here at Robin Hoods Bay. Behind the tall narrow cottages are handsome eighteenth-century mansions once owned by the whaling captains. The houses, which cling precariously to the side of the cliff, are reached by narrow alleys and steps, and in bygone days smugglers unloaded their contraband on the beach and carried it to the top of the village through a maze of secret tunnels between the tightly packed houses.

Below
Whitby, where the *Endeavour* moors each year and attracts thousands of visitors, is still a working fishing port and boats can be seen unloading their catches at the harbour. A fish quay, built in the lower harbour and complete with fish sheds and offices, is the venue for the sale and auction of the day's catch.

NORTH YORKSHIRE COAST

9 Scarborough

The stunning view over the great curved South Bay at Scarborough is unrivalled. The harbour dates from 1225, when Henry III made a grant of forty oaks from his royal forests to the men of Scarborough to use in the harbour. A royal charter of 1251 stated: 'It is for the benefit of the Town of Scardeburgh to make a certain new port with timber and stone towards the sea whereby all ships arriving thither may enter and sail out without danger as well at the beginning of Flood as at High water'.

'Scarborough, though a paltry town,' wrote the novelist Tobias Smollett in 1771, 'is romantic from its situation along a cliff that overlaps the sea.' Far from being a 'paltry town', Scarborough has immense character with great scenic beauty, historic sites and extravagant amusements. It is an ideal family resort. There are sands to the north, sands to the south, and inland that huge basin — the Vale of Pickering. There are the remains of the magnificent twelfth-century castle, dominating the jutting limestone headland. There are interesting alleyways by the harbour, the Spa, the cast-iron Cliff Bridge, lengthy promenades, a great Gothic seaside hotel, Peasholm Park, a fine Victorian theatre, a wonderfully varied seafront crammed with cafés, souvenir shops and arcades, and the funicular cliff lifts, connecting the beaches to the town high above.

It was only when my second son, Matthew, was studying for a fine art degree at Leeds University that I discovered the church of St Martin-on-the-Hill. Matthew introduced me to this hidden gem. Behind an unprepossessing Victorian exterior is a church which boasts a magnificent display of decorative work and stained glass. William Morris, Ford Madox Brown, Dante Gabriel Rossetti, Edward Burne-Jones and Philip Webb, the greatest of the Pre-Raphaelite artists and craftsmen, combined to produce the stunning interior.

Scarborough is home for Alan Ayckbourn's brilliant plays, performed at the splendid Stephen Joseph Theatre. One abiding memory was when, a couple of years ago, I appeared at the theatre and later signed books in the foyer. An elderly woman in a thick headscarf approached.

'Are you anybody?' asked the woman.

'No', I replied.

'Have you been on anything?' she asked.

'No', I replied.

'What's the book about?'

I told her it was an amusing account of my life as a school inspector in the Dales, with no sex, violence or bad language.

The woman smiled sympathetically and shook her head. 'It'll not sell, love', she told me, before departing. Yorkshire people are not noted for their tact.

Scarborough Castle dominates the town and harbour 300 feet (90 m) below. This mighty fortress, set high on the cliff, is naturally defended and a perfect lookout spot, and was a strategically important northern base of monarchs for five centuries. The first stone fortress, built in the twelfth century by William le Gros, and later extended and fortified by Henry II, survived until the seventeenth century, when it was badly damaged during Civil War sieges.

I have many happy childhood memories of Scarborough. A walk to the lighthouse at the end of Vincents Pier with my father to watch the boats coming into the harbour was an annual event.

Above
The Grand Hotel, Scarborough, is one of Britain's most magnificent Victorian Gothic seaside hotels. This 'calendar' building, conceived by the designer of Leeds Town Hall, Cuthbert Brodrick, has a room for every day of the year, a floor for every day of the week and a domed tower for each season.

Right
This spectacular view over Scarborough from Castle Hill shows a vast summer sky and the sea at its mildest. Beautiful and tranquil it may be, but I like Scarborough the best in winter, when icy gales pound the harbour and the sea is a forest of white crests.

SCARBOROUGH

10 *Helmsley and Rievaulx*

A stunning view across the lake at Castle Howard, with Sir John Vanbrugh's first masterpiece — a vast and imposing palace — a shadowy outline in the distance. Designed for Charles Howard, the third earl of Carlisle, and begun in 1700, Castle Howard was the setting for the television series *Brideshead Revisited*.

On the edge of the North York Moors National Park, by the banks of the River Rye, is Helmsley with its orange roofs, old coaching inns, impressive half-timbered rectory and the gaunt round ruins of the twelfth-century castle, battered in the Civil War by Lord Fairfax.

The extensive grounds of the beautifully restored Duncombe Park with its fine landscaped terrace, sweep up to within a few yards of the market place with its astonishingly ornate Gothic memorial.

To the west of Helmsley rise the beautiful remains of Rievaulx Abbey, standing amongst the wooded hills. This was the first substantial Cistercian abbey in Yorkshire, founded in 1132 and, despite centuries of plunder (many of the houses in the village of Rievaulx were built from stone salvaged from the abbey), it is still remarkably complete. Enough remains of the building to give a clear view of how vast and impressive the abbey used to be. Looking down on the extensive remains is Rievaulx Terrace, a grassy promenade built around 1758, with views of the abbey, and a vast panorama along the Rye Valley and to the undulating hills beyond.

Bilsdale, the long valley which stretches from Helmsley in the south and towards Stokesley in the north, has been farmed up to the moorland tops since the monks of Rievaulx settled there. Only a few scattered farms can be seen today, but there is the tiny village of Chop Gate. I once spoke at the Chop Gate Village Hall on a dark, windy and very wet evening. 'I'm delighted to be here at Chop Gate', I began. 'Chop Yat!' chorused my audience loudly.

From Helmsley, the Cleveland Way, a 109-mile (174 km) trail, meanders through the moorland scenery of the Hambleton and Cleveland hills, ending at Filey Brigg. Unlike my brother-in-law, a seasoned walker who has completed the trek in one go, I opt to avoid the aches and the blisters by walking it in easy stages.

The Reverend Laurence Sterne, novelist, wit and *bon viveur*, lived in Coxwold, a delightful village situated south-west of Helmsley. My English teacher at A-level, the wonderful Miss Mary Wainwright, would certainly not have approved of the vicar's taste for high living — wine, gambling, hunting, horse racing and cock fighting — but she considered his picaresque novel *The Life and Opinions of Tristram Shandy, Gentleman* to be one of the comic classics of English literature.

Little remains of the once-fine fortress at Helmsley. Following a three-month siege during the Civil War, Colonel Jordan Crossland, a loyal supporter of Charles I, surrendered to Sir Thomas Fairfax, commander of the Parliamentarian army. The Roundheads demolished enough of the castle to ensure it could never be used again, but failed to blow up the Norman keep. The eastern wall still stands to an impressive height of ninety-seven feet (30 m), giving some idea of what the castle once looked like.

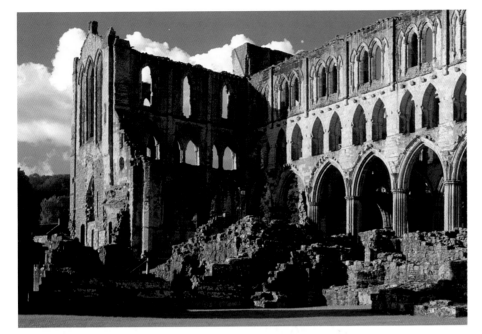

Rievaulx Abbey was founded in 1132, and building work had begun by about 1140. It took its name from a direct translation of the French meaning 'Rye Vale'. Today the ancient imposing walls stand in a sheltered and tranquil valley, surrounded by manicured lawns, neat copses and lush meadows, but when Walter Espec encouraged a group of French monks to found an abbey, the land was said to be fit for only 'wild beasts and robbers'. There would have been over 100 monks and as many as 600 lay brothers in this community at one time who, by rearing sheep, grinding corn and smelting iron, became immensely wealthy.

The gaunt remains of Byland Abbey, near Coxwold, are still wonderfully majestic and evocative. The dramatic cream ashlar sandstone façade, with the twenty-six foot (8 m) diameter rose window, rises to its full height, and shows how huge and impressive the building must have been. Byland Abbey was one of the biggest Cistercian houses of its time, with the largest cloisters of any Yorkshire abbey. Work began in 1177 by former brothers of the Order of Savigny — which had recently merged with the Cistercian Order — who were attracted to the wild secluded river valley where they could raise sheep and pray in peace.

A 'host of golden daffodils' border the path leading up to Kilburn Parish Church. Many examples of the work of Robert Thompson, the woodcarver and master craftsman, are found here, where a chapel was dedicated to the 'Mouseman' shortly before his death in 1955. Thompson's work is characterised by sturdy designs, the dark tones of the wood and the rippled effect left by the arched cutting blade of the adze.

The White Horse of Kilburn, carved into the oolitic limestone of Whitestonecliffe, gazes down from the heights of Roulston Scar above the villages of Kilburn and Coxwold. The hill figure, cut into the turf by the teacher John Hodgson and his pupils in 1857, is a landmark for miles around.

Facing page
On the River Rye is the handsome town of Helmsley. which marks the western end of the Cleveland Way. Red roofs, a rushing river, ancient inns, impressive stone houses, the old market cross on its stepped base and the generous square (pictured) make it, for me, the finest market town in Yorkshire.

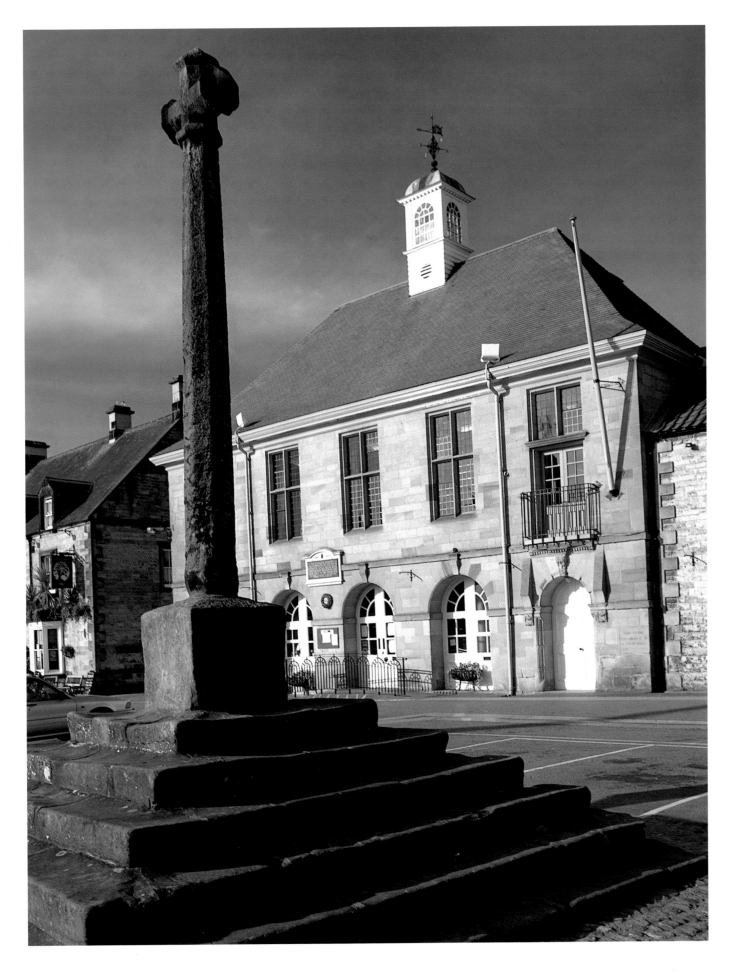

79

Left
Between Thirsk and Helmsley rises
Sutton Bank, 'Gateway to the North
York Moors'. The panorama from
the viewpoint at the very top must
rank as one of the finest in Britain.

Above
There is an awesome pulling power
in these iron monsters standing and
steaming in a rank at the Pickering
Traction Engine Rally. The event,
which has taken place for over fifty
years, is the largest gathering of steam
and vintage engines in the North.

11 *North York Moors*

In *The Other Side of the Dale*, I related a conversation I had had with a grizzled old farmer, who described the bogs of the moorland heights on Egton Moor in graphic detail: 'Go off t' road and tha'll end up, up to thee neck in peaty slime, that'll drag thee to thy death inch by inch. Whole flocks o' sheep have disappeared up theer, tha knaws, and t' shepherd were nivver seen agean neither.' The peat bogs and marshes are indeed bleak and treacherous, but there is an austere beauty about them.

The single biggest attraction in the North York Moors National Park is the North Yorkshire Moors Railway.

An eighteen-mile (29 km) track takes passengers from Pickering northwards and into the heart of the moors, through a deep glacial channel and the spectacular steep-sided gorge at Newton Dale, and on to the northern terminus at Grosmont.

The Pickering to Whitby line was opened in 1836 after consultation with the engineer George Stephenson. An army of navvies had taken three years to hack out the route though the inhospitable, rugged terrain. At first, carriages were horse drawn and trundled along the track at ten miles (16 km) per hour. In 1847 the first steam train chugged along and, for the next hundred and some years, the railway transported ironstone goods and then visitors who could escape the pollution of the towns and cities to enjoy the breathtaking scenic journey across the moors. In 1965 came the infamous Beeching 'axe' and the section of line between Pickering and Grosmont was closed.

Yorkshire people have a dogged determination — some would say stubbornness. Two years after the closure, a group of passionate railway enthusiasts formed the North Yorkshire Moors Railway Preservation Society and raised funds to purchase the trackbed from British Rail. The line and the stations along it were lovingly restored, and the line was partially reopened in 1969 and fully reopened in 1973. We should be massively grateful for such custodians who guard, treasure and cherish a priceless heritage. Without the efforts of the North Yorkshire Moors Railway Preservation Society and other interested parties, young people would never experience at first hand those gleaming locomotives, smelling of oil, putting out clouds of steam as they race down the track.

A steam locomotive speeds down the track at Darnholme (meaning 'dark meadow'), a hamlet between Grosmont and Goathland. This stretch of the North Yorkshire Moors Railway, with a gradient of one in forty-nine, has one of the steepest inclines of any railway track in the country.

Below
There is a green, sheltered softness about Westerdale in the Esk Valley. Surrounded on all sides by rough moorland and scattered with an attractive assortment of farmhouses, cottages and barns, it is a quiet dale tucked away in the heart of the North York Moors.

A locomotive, shrouded in smoke, chugs out of Grosmont Station. The village of Grosmont, situated in the exquisite Esk Valley and close to the confluence of the Murk Esk with the River Esk, takes its name from the small priory founded around 1200. The beautifully neat and clean station bears witness to the dedication of the railway enthusiasts who maintain it.

Below
Danby Dale is a landscape of strong shades: black hawthorn hedges, walls of square, deep stone, little copses of dark green and grey farmsteads. Here is moorland scenery at its best. The Moors Centre at Danby is housed in a former shooting lodge set in thirteen acres (5 ha) of riverside, meadow, formal gardens and picnic areas.

Sheep graze by Hutton Beck, the little watercourse which trickles through Hutton-le-Hole, arguably Yorkshire's prettiest village. Cottages of mellow local stone and houses of discrete grey are grouped around the village green which is the size of a meadow. In the centre of the village is the Ryedale Folk Museum, which houses a fascinating collection of artefacts. The small church has fine oak furniture made by Robert 'Mouseman' Thompson of Kilburn.

Below
In the nineteenth century, Beck Hole was a bustling centre for ironstone mining; today, industry has gone, and life is tranquil and unhurried.

In the heart of the North York Moors is the picturesque village of Goathland. Grassy fields and verges, cropped by black-faced moorland sheep, sweep up directly onto the heather and bracken of the moors. In recent years this quiet village has achieved fame as the location for the popular television series *Heartbeat*.

12 *Hull and Holderness*

This masterpiece of creative and civil engineering — the Humber Bridge — was opened by the Queen on the 17th July 1981. It took eight years to construct at a cost of £151 million and was, for seventeen years, the world's largest single-span suspension bridge. On the 4,620 foot (1,410 m) main span, enough steel cable was used to stretch one and a half times around the world.

'From Hell, Hull and Halifax, Good Lord deliver us' goes the *Thieves Litany*, rather unkindly. Dominic, my third son, studied at the University of Hull, so I came to know well this great city, which extends for a remarkable seven miles (11 km) along the Humber with ten miles (16 km) of quays. In 1293, Edward I, recognising a good thing when he saw it, acquired this strategic port of entry on the River Humber from the monks of Meaux Abbey (at a royal discount, of course). He gave the settlement the title of 'Kinges town upon Hull'.

There is much to see in Hull: museums and art galleries, historic houses and churches, attractive open spaces and heritage trails along the city's dramatic waterfront. Highlights for me are the Wilberforce House Museum, which presents in graphic detail the appalling history of the slave trade; the Town Docks Museum; the Streetlife Transport Museum; and the Spurn Lightship moored in the Marina. The Deep, which tells the story of the world's oceans, and is home for seven species of shark, conger eels, rays and thousands of stunning sea creatures, is an awesome experience.

The road north to Hull leads to the spectacular Humber Bridge, the world's third longest single-span bridge, with an overall length of 2,430 yards (2,220 m). Four huge concrete pillars, spanned with thin wired-steel cables, rise 500 feet (152 m) from the water.

'For those who do not know this town, there is a great surprise in store', the poet laureate John Betjeman said of Beverley. The oldest town in East Yorkshire, Beverley is one of the county's most intriguing places, with a grand Gothic Minster in glowing limestone which rivals York, a market cross, guildhall and medieval gatehouse, galleries, museums and heritage walks. The Beverley Festival, one of the main events in the vibrant Yorkshire arts calendar, takes place in June.

To the east of the town is Holderness, with a landscape unique in Yorkshire. This wide empty plain, constantly eroded by the North Sea, is a strange and lonely land, scoured and bleached but with a particular beauty.

Hull's importance as a port dates from the thirteenth century. It became the premier port for handling England's wool trade in the fourteenth century, and in the sixteenth became a major centre for the timber trade. Hull still remains a major conduit, handling about a sixth of the nation's seaborne trade, but the fishing industry has greatly declined. In 1866 over 300 trawlers were based in Hull or on the Humber. Now, sadly, there are very few.

The impetus for Hull's dockland development came in 1774 when an act was passed giving the go-ahead for the construction of a dock. Completed in 1778, this vast area of water space — 600 yards (550 m) long and 85 yards (78 m) wide, and with a total area of eleven acres (4.5 ha) — was the biggest of its kind in Britain and transformed the city into England's third most important port. Today Hull has seven miles (11 km) of dock facilities, including warehouses and wharves, and twelve miles (19 km) of quays, and handles £1,000 million worth of cargo each year.

Below

This substantial red-brick house, 25 High Street in Hull, was built in the 1660s in the Artisan Mannerist style. It was here, in 1759, that William Wilberforce was born. At the age of twenty-one, this great social reformer was elected to parliament to represent the city and it was due to his untiring efforts that, in 1807, a bill was carried for the abolition of slavery in this country. But the barbaric trade in human cargo continued in the British colonies until 1833, when an act to abolish slavery in the colonies was passed — just a few days before Wilberforce's death. His statue outside the house has beneath it the words: 'England owes to him the reformation of manners, the world owes to him the abolition of slavery'.

Right
It may come as a surprise to learn that this palatial three-domed building once served as the Town Docks Offices. It is now the Hull Maritime Museum, and houses a unique collection of paintings, artefacts, models and relics which trace Hull's colourful maritime history.

Below
South of Withernsea there stretches a desolate spit of flat windswept dunes known as Spurn Point. This narrow hook of ever-shifting sand and shingle, that curls around the mouth of the Humber Estuary, is a dramatic and daunting place.

13 Harrogate and Knaresborough

Harlow Carr Gardens near Harrogate is the Royal Horticultural Society's testing place for plants. It does not have formally laid-out gardens, but trial and demonstration areas, which nurture a great variety of herbs and plants, including the national collection of rhubarb.

On his visit to Harrogate in 1858, Charles Dickens described this amazing town as 'the queerest place, with the strangest people in it, leading the oddest lives'. Here is opulence on a grand scale: luxury hotels like the Majestic and the Crown, the Classical Spa Rooms, the Royal Baths and Pump Room, the Kursaal or Royal Hall, the Westminster Arcade, the Grand Opera House (now Harrogate Theatre), the magnificent Valley Gardens and the famous Stray. At every turn are turrets, towers and massive facades. Even the water towers are adorned with pilasters and classical motifs, and topped by intricate ironwork.

It was the discovery of curative waters which transformed Harrogate from an obscure village into the 'World's Greatest Spa'. In the eighteenth and nineteenth centuries, huge villas were built, a racecourse was developed, public amenities such as the Assembly Rooms and the Sulphur Well Temple were built, and visitors flooded in (excuse the pun) to take the waters. Today Harrogate retains its appeal and ranks as one of Britain's most attractive towns, full of character and colour, and the venue for many conferences and national events.

Nearby Knaresborough, with its elegant houses clustering around the dramatic cliffs of the Nidd Gorge, is well worth a visit. The ruins of the fourteenth-century castle, a former royal residence, tower above the town. 'The castle standeth magnificently and strongly as rok', wrote John Leland in the sixteenth century. Close by is the handsome market place with its classical town hall. The market dates from the fourteenth century, and some of the buildings in the market place may well have their origins in that century. Three most interesting places to visit are Mother Shipton's Cave, where personal items, hanging beneath dripping ledges, have been literally petrified by the limestone content; the Chapel of Our Lady of the Crag, an ancient wayside shrine cut out of solid rock; and the modern arts centre.

Part of Harrogate's enduring charm is in its well-tended gardens and public spaces. Everywhere in this spacious and elegant spa town are colourful plants, bright flowers and green lawns. In spring and autumn, when the annual Harrogate Flower Shows takes place, the town looks particularly beautiful.

The great viaduct at Knaresborough spans the tranquil River Nidd, which has cut deep into the limestone to create the cliffs on which this fascinating town stands. The viaduct dates from 1851, and replaced the original viaduct of 1848 which collapsed into the river before it was finished.

14 *Fountains Abbey and Ripon*

One of the classical statues near the waterside temple at Studley Royal, the estate adjoining Fountains Abbey created in the early eighteenth century. The formality of the park entrance is maintained along the half-mile (0.8 km) walk to the abbey, past neat lawns, water gardens, landscaped vistas and well-tended shrubberies.

Ripon, the second-smallest city in England, was one of the most important coaching stations along the Great North Road. It has a spacious market square, which Daniel Defoe declared to be the most beautiful in England, an impressive classical town hall, elegant red-brick houses, splendid shops, homely inns and a magnificent cathedral. A well-established community lived here in medieval times when three hospitals were built, but the city's growth rested on its place as a commercial centre, trading in textiles, leather and livestock.

The Cathedral Church of St Peter and St Wilfrid, with its imposing gabled and turreted west front, dates from the seventh century, when St Wilfrid built a crypt as part of the monastery. The tiny room, the oldest complete Saxon crypt in England, was not intended for services but for pilgrims wishing to view the relics.

Ripon is an ideal centre for the visitor to explore one of Yorkshire's most interesting areas. At Kilburn, in 1857, the schoolmaster and his pupils carved the great White Horse on Roulston Moor (I wonder what the Victorian school inspectors made of that project), and it was here the distinguished woodcarver Robert Thompson, the 'mouse man', was born and established his workshop. I remember being taken round Ampleforth College by a pupil who was quite the expert on 'Mousy' Thompson. The college, he told me, has the largest of his oak tables — quite a magnificent piece of furniture.

Fountains Abbey, the largest monastic ruin in Britain, and the Studley Royal estate, a great eighteenth-century green garden with formal lawns, waterside temple and well-tended shrubberies, are but a few miles away. Brimham Rocks, fifty acres (20 ha) of weird and wonderful weathered outcrops, is within easy travelling distance, and 'twixt Ripon and Harrogate is Ripley, with a castle full of interest and a church housing a unique 'weeping cross'.

The Cathedral of St Peter and St Wilfrid at Ripon, which stands commandingly above the Ure Valley, had once a dark and dismal façade, but after careful restoration and cleaning it now sparkles in the sunlight. St Wilfrid, who became abbot of a monastery in Ripon in AD 660, soon after established a church. The Saxon crypt, built by him in AD 672 for pilgrims to view the relics, survives to this day and is one of only six remaining in England. The church was rebuilt in the twelfth century, the finest feature being the dazzling west front, with its five bays of lancets.

Fountains Abbey is without doubt the best preserved and most complete of all English abbeys. It was in 1132 that 13 Benedictine monks were granted wild and inhospitable land in a valley bottom by Thurstan, the archbishop of York. This was Skelldale, 'a place remote from all the world, uninhabited, set with thorns … fit more, it seemed, for the dens of wild beasts than for the uses of mankind'. The majority of the buildings were completed by the mid-thirteenth century. The cellarium (pictured) remains remarkably intact after nearly nine centuries.

The ceiling of St Mary's Church at Studley Royal is a masterpiece of Victorian ecclesiastical art. The architect, William Burges, designed a dramatic Gothic church, and the intricately decorated interior is characteristic of the High Church religious revival of this period.

Close to Ripon and set in award-winning gardens is the elegant Newby Hall, the splendid seventeenth-century country house commissioned by Sir Edward Blackett. The interior ranks as perhaps the finest example of Robert Adam's work, and includes a fine collection of classical sculptures.

Ripley Castle, between Harrogate and Ripon, has lost its fortress-like appearance over the years. The short tower block, which was part of the original house, has a priest's hole, and a large upper room boasts a fine plaster Jacobean ceiling. The grounds were laid out by Capability Brown.

15 Upper Nidderdale

The growth of the textile industry in the nineteenth century meant a considerable amount of water was required. As a consequence, four reservoirs were constructed in upper Nidderdale; Angram, completed in 1919 and pictured here, being the highest. This great expanse of water, situated below Great Whernside in Nidderdale, is a mile (1.6 km) long, a third of a mile (0.5 km) wide, with a depth of over 100 feet (30 m). The reservoir, surrounded by a wild, rugged and remote land, is in an Area of Outstanding Natural Beauty.

In 2002 I was asked to write the forward to *Nidderdale, Land in Our Blood: a Portrait of Life and Landscape in a Yorkshire Dale*. This is a splendid collection of photographs produced by Paul Harris and the students of Nidderdale High School and Community College. The collection provides a unique perspective of the diverse groups who live and work in the dale. I was particularly delighted to take on this pleasant task because, of all the dales, this winding valley, some twenty-five miles (40 km) long and carved out of Millstone Grit, is my favourite, and I have many fond memories of this spectacular part of the county, and of the teachers and children I encountered in the schools there.

On my travels as a school inspector up to Pateley Bridge from Harrogate, through Ripley and Glasshouses and on to Lofthouse in the valley bottom, I would marvel at the panoramic views which stretched before me: soft green pastures dotted with sheep; heavy square-bodied Highland cattle; a vast sky streaked with creamy clouds; nestling, sunlit farmsteads and craggy gritstone walls. It has, no doubt, remained the same for centuries.

Near Middlesmoor, with its quaint corners and cobbles, is the impressive How Stean Gorge, thick with lichen, ferns and mosses growing beside the clear waters and copses of ash, hazel and oak trees. This is Yorkshire's Little Switzerland.

I felt in Nidderdale, of all the Dales, a great sense of tranquillity and timelessness around me, as if the noises and concerns of the modern world had been swallowed up by those rolling fields.

Surrounding Greenhow is a bleak and desolate moorland, pock-marked by years of intensive mining. The area evolved from leadmining in the seventeenth century, and a community grew up. The ruins of the miners' houses can still be seen. Halliwell Sutcliffe in his classic work *The Striding Dales* describes the road from Pateley Bridge to Greenhow, bordered by 'lonely acres ... shelterless to winter gales and August's torrid heat ... It is a strange desolate country this of Greenhow, whose loneliness seems only deepened by the unsheltered road that winds through it, a narrow ribbon of grey.'

The hillside village of Middlesmoor, standing 950 feet (290 m) above sea level, has changed little over the years and has certainly remained unspoilt. With its solid stone houses, quaint cottages and cobbled ways, it is one of Nidderdale's gems. The view from the churchyard of St Chad's is spectacular.

Opposite
This hardy black-faced Swaledale ewe, with her lambs, is at home on the fells and moorland. Swaledale sheep live with ease in the exposed climate of the Pennines. Ewes are brought down to the valleys only at lambing times to give birth in the fields near farm buildings, and are then driven back on the hills. In early summer there are as many as half a million ewes and lambs in the Yorkshire Dales National Park.

To the east of Pateley Bridge in Nidderdale, on the edge of high heathland, are Brimham Rocks, a fantastic collection of eroded stones. Centuries of wind and rain have sculptured these weird outcrops of exposed millstone grit into curious shapes. Some rise up as tall columns, others (like the one pictured) stand precariously balanced, and several appear like carved animals: a dancing bear, an elephant, a frog, a tortoise and a tiger.

GERVASE PHINN'S YORKSHIRE

16 Malhamdale

Lazy-looking sheep crop the rich pastures on a mild spring day.

I was seventeen when I first saw Malham Cove. My geography master Mr Taylor had organised a sixth-form field trip for us to study limestone scenery. I had read about 'clints' and 'grykes', limestone pavements and caverns, potholes and subterranean rivers in wearisome detail in my dog-eared copy of *Physical Geography*. Horrocks' dull prose had not prepared me for what I was to see.

We approached by a footpath from the south and an immense bow-shaped cove came into view. It was breathtaking. I had never seen anything quite as bleak and rugged. Formed millions of years ago, when the earth's crust cracked, fracturing the rock so that it dropped vertically, Malham Cove belies description. Around 240 feet (80 m) high, a thousand feet (300 m) wide, it forms a spectacular and unique natural feature. Once a huge crashing waterfall cascaded over the vertical cliff, creating a fall higher than Niagara.

We spent a week at the youth hostel in the ancient village of Malham, in walking distance of the National Park Information Centre and, more importantly, the two friendly inns, surrounded by domed hills, limestone cliffs and the broad acres of Malham Moor. That week we saw bubbling springs and cataracts, crags and scars — stone-weathered, bone-white and shiny as marble — ravines and overhanging cliffs, and the spectacular Malham Tarn, one of only two natural lakes in the Yorkshire Dales, about half a mile square (1.3 km²) and fourteen feet (4 m) deep.

That week I thought of my mother and the story she had read to me of Tom, the little chimney sweep who meets the babies in the cool, clear water. I learnt on that first visit to Malham that Charles Kingsley, having passed through Bradford and witnessed the squalor and dirt, visited Tarn House in 1858 as the guest of the millionaire philanthropist Walter Morrison. He must have been struck by the stark contrast of the dark industrial city and the stunning limestone scenery. Kingsley was a skilled botanist and was reputedly asked to explain the streaks of black on the face of the cove. He explained that they were made by a little chimney sweep slipping over the clifftop and sliding down into the stream. Here was his inspiration for the classic fantasy story *The Water-Babies*.

This striking limestone scenery in
upper Wharfedale is the result of
the variable weather conditions and
centuries of erosion. A limestone
pavement of humps and fissures
('clints' and 'grykes') has been
fractured by frost, polished by ice
and dissolved by rain.

GERVASE PHINN'S YORKSHIRE

Here is nature in all her glory. The wide bare surface of the limestone pavement above Malham Cove, crinkled and weather-scoured, contrasts with the soft rounded shoulders of the rolling hills beyond.

Below
I shared Adam Walker's amazement when I first came upon Gordale Scar. 'Good heavens!' he exclaimed in 1779. 'What was my astonishment! If you would conceive it properly, depend upon neither pen nor pencil for 'tis impossible to give you an adequate idea of it.'

Opposite
Malhamdale has a fine network of green lanes, once used by cattle drovers. Here a limestone lane, sun-bleached to the whiteness of bone and bordered by seemingly endless drystone walls, leads down into Malham village. Bill Bryson declared this part of Yorkshire 'my favourite view in the world'.

GERVASE PHINN'S YORKSHIRE

MALHAMDALE

17 *Wensleydale*

Bolton Castle in Wensleydale, the formidable fourteenth-century fortress, was said to be more comfortable and spacious than earlier built castles. This great thrusting pile of masonry, still stout-walled and with windows like sightless eyes, must have appeared bleak and intimidating to the sad Scottish queen who was imprisoned here from July 1568 to January 1569.

I was once told by a grizzled old farmer that the county of Yorkshire is bigger than Israel and covers more acres than letters in the King James Bible. It may be something of an exaggeration (although Yorkshire folk are not prone to embellishing), but the county is certainly large.

It is in winter, when the strings of caravans and 'off-comed-uns' have disappeared, and only a few hardy red-faced ramblers can be seen striding the fells, that the vastness and beauty of the Dales fill me with a real sense of wonder.

My first visit to Wensleydale was in winter. From Bedale to Leyburn and then on to Redmire and Hawes, following the course of the River Ure, I travelled for mile upon mile without seeing a soul — just the tumbling acres of dark green flecked with snow, deep valleys, woodland and craggy outcrops, drystone walls, barns and bridges, churches and long grey farmhouses, through villages which appeared so much a part of the landscape and which had changed very little over the centuries.

I returned to Wensleydale the following spring and how different it was. Beneath a vast blank curve of blue there stretched the brilliant greens of the pastureland, rolling and billowing up to the richer darker hues of the far-off fells. Fat, creamy sheep grazed lazily behind white-silvered limestone walls, while their lambs frisked and raced. There was a heady scent of May blossom blending with the smells of earth and grass.

Those who like me are fans of James Herriot will want to visit Askrigg where much of the BBC television series *All Creatures Great and Small* was filmed. There is also the busy market town of Hawes, home of the Dales Countryside Museum and its fascinating collections of farming and household implements, donated by those redoubtable chroniclers of the Dales (and Wensleydale residents) Marie Hartley and Joan Ingilby.

But for me the special qualities of Wensleydale are its vastness and beauty, the stark contrasts and the sense of timelessness. There are few other landscapes in England to rival its infinite variety.

Below
Askrigg was granted a market charter
by Queen Elizabeth I in 1587. The
stepped market cross, set in a cobbled
area outside the church, is a reminder
of former times when the village was
a busy commercial centre, famous for
knitting, dyeing, brewing and lead
trading. Sadly, there is no longer a
market here. The impressive fifteenth-
century church of St Oswald stands
proudly in the centre of this distinctive
Dales village, and opposite is the house
used as the exterior of James Herriot's
home and surgery in the television
series *All Creatures Great and Small*.

Opposite
In the heart of the Dales is West Burton, one of Wensleydale's most picturesque villages. Burton comes from the Old English word *burhtun*, meaning fortified place. The village grew around the central green, where a thriving weekly market used to take place. Just to the east of the village, a scenic path leads across a small packhorse bridge to Cauldron Falls, perhaps the most striking of all Wensleydale's waterfalls.

Below
This terraced cottage, with steps leading to the second floor, is in the unspoilt and peaceful village of Thornton Rust in Wensleydale. From the cluster of attractive stone cottages, neat houses and farms, the wide main street rises up to the fells where there are spectacular views over Bishopdale and Wensleydale.

Above
A drystone wall, one of the most striking features of the rural landscape, climbs effortlessly across an empty field towards Addlebrough. This flat-topped limestone summit looming over Askrigg was used by the Romans as a lookout station, and an Ancient British chieftain is thought to be buried here.

Right
Morning mist shrouds Wensleydale, giving this most beautiful fertile vale, bounded by soft green hills, a kind of ethereal splendour.

WENSLEYDALE

An ash tree in all its grandeur flourishes in the rich soil of Walden Beck Dale. This steep and lonely valley is an Environmentally Sensitive Area, and sympathetic farming methods have nurtured the growth of wild flowers and encouraged an amazing variety of wildlife.

Facing page
Three distinct cascades — upper, middle and lower — comprise the spectacular Aysgarth Falls. Gushing water bubbles and froths over a series of stepped limestone ridges along as dramatic half mile (0.8 km) of the River Ure in Wensleydale.

WENSLEYDALE

18 *Swaledale*

The secluded mountain splendour of verdant woodland, cascading water and rippling pools in the exquisite Kisdon Gorge, a dramatic steep-sided valley at the head of Swaledale between Keld and Muker.

There is breathtaking beauty in the hay meadows of Wensleydale, where buttercups and clover blaze along the valley bottoms. There is a simple pastoral beauty in the close-cropped sheep pastures of Ribblesdale, smooth and soft as a billiard table, where rock rose and mountain pansy flourish. The Yorkshire Dales is indeed a land of contrasts, and this is seen in no better landscape than Swaledale. Here is a land of beautiful valleys and vast empty moorland, soaring fells and wind-scoured crags, dark scattered woodland and deep carved gorges, bubbling becks and tumbling waterfalls.

Apart from the stunning scenery, there is so much to see in Swaledale. There are the beautiful villages of Thwaite and Muker in the upper dale, Gunnerside with its leadminers' cottages, and Reeth with its inns and houses clustered round a sloping village green. The Tan Hill Inn near Keld, at the head of Swaledale, is the highest pub in Britain (it stands at 1,732 feet/523 m)

Richmond is a market town not to be missed. There are the fine thirteenth-century wall paintings at St Agatha's Church at nearby Easby; the museum of the Green Howards Regiment, housed in the old Holy Trinity Church in the market square; the magnificent Norman castle, the earliest in Yorkshire to be built wholly in stone from the beginning; and, of course, the gem of the town — the Georgian Theatre, the second-oldest working theatre in the country, built in 1788 by actor/manager Samuel Butler, and once heated by open fires and lit by candlelight. The theatre still survives in its original form, and today is a treasured part of our cultural heritage.

Richmond's distinctive cobbled market place at Richmond viewed from the castle. This is one of Yorkshire's most impressive towns, rich in interesting and unusual buildings. Here are the Green Howards Regimental Museum, the magnificent castle and, of course, the famous Georgian Theatre.

Clustered around a bend in the road is the compact and unpretentious village of Thwaite in upper Swaledale. To the south, a road climbs to the fells where there are superb uninterrupted views over Cliff Beck and towards Buttertubs Pass, so called from the distinctive fluted limestone potholes found there.

'O! I would send you this today —
The peace of the hills, and sweet on the wind
The scent of hay.'
(*Poems* by Joan Ingilby, 1984)

What could be more inspiring for the
poet than this view over a hay meadow
at Keld?

Facing page
Nestling below rounded-shouldered
hills, and above Straw Beck near to its
confluence with the Swale, sits Muker.
The view down the green lane is typical
of much Dales village scenery —
clustered cottages, flowering verges
and a green hillside beyond.

GERVASE PHINN'S YORKSHIRE

Below
A lonely barn, its stone slate roof covered in a light dusting of snow, stands beneath the vast empty moorland, soaring fells and wind-scoured crags in Swaledale. It is estimated that there are over 1,000 field barns in Swaledale, built between 1750 and the end of the nineteenth century. The Yorkshire Dales National Park Authority created an innovative conservation project in 1989 to help farmers repair and preserve these unique buildings.

130

GERVASE PHINN'S YORKSHIRE

19 Ilkley and Skipton

Prince Charles visited Skipton's Victorian-style covered shopping arcade in March 1988 and was agreeably impressed. In his book *A Vision of Britain* he wrote of the architecture: 'I rather like the way the developers have roofed over an old street and made it resemble an arcade. Critics will mutter "pastiche" knowingly, but it's proving a great success.' The courtyard is the venue for seasonal entertainment — morris dancers, brass bands and carol singers.

Skipton, the 'Gateway to the Dales', lies in the Aire Gap, a natural break in the Pennines. The bustling market town is dominated by the castle, former home of the powerful Clifford family, and one of the most complete and well-preserved medieval fortresses in the country. In addition to an immense banqueting hall, there is a series of kitchens with original fittings, a Tudor courtyard and an impressive fourteenth-century gateway carrying the Clifford family motto '*Desormais*', meaning 'Henceforth'.

At the top of the high street, near the castle, stands the parish church of the Holy Trinity with its beautiful oak roof and treasury of artefacts, interesting tombs and memorials.

North of Skipton is the village of Rylstone, once the home of the influential and unfortunate Norton family. Wordsworth, who found great inspiration wandering among Craven's mountain tracts, tells the legend of Francis Norton, who was murdered and buried at Bolton Priory, in his poem *The White Doe of Rylestone*, which he felt to be 'in conception the highest work I have produced'.

The Wharfedale town of Ilkley, with its fine residences and villas, cafés and tea-rooms, tree-lined avenues, varied shops and pleasant gardens, attracts many visitors. More famous than the town itself, however, is Ilkley Moor, immortalised in Yorkshire's best-known song. On a bright summer day the heather-clad moor looks peaceful and welcoming, but in winter it can be the darkest and most forbidding place on earth.

I had the great pleasure some years ago of sharing a platform at the Ilkley Literary Festival with Jim Wight, son of the great James Herriot. He told the story of a farmer, who, having read one of his father's books, concluded: 'It's all nowt about owt'. I had a similar experience in Ilkley when I was signing books after my talk. I was approached by a rather disgruntled-looking ex-teacher who announced: 'I was going to write your book, but you got there first'.

Facing page
In the centre of Skipton is the half-mile (0.8 km) Springs branch of the Leeds-Liverpool Canal. Built for Lord Thanet in the eighteenth century to bring goods and raw materials into the town and limestone from his quarries, it runs from the main canal around the back of Skipton Castle to a former stone-loading wharf. Boats were loaded from a chute which can still be seen at the far end of Springs Canal.

A tall mill chimney towers above a branch of the Leeds-Liverpool Canal at Shipley. This impressive stretch of water, now busy with barges and waterbuses, was the first of three canals built to transport goods across the Pennines. Construction began in 1773 but the project, which involved the building of ninety-one locks, was only completed in 1816.

A secluded path winds through
Middleton Wood, north of Ilkley.
This dense woodland is a naturalists'
paradise: in spring, a carpet of bluebells;
in summer, a tapestry of red campions,
yellow archangels and white starry
stitchworts; and in autumn a blaze
of coloured leafage.

The still water at Embsay Reservoir in Craven glistens like ice. This huge expanse, completed in 1907, retains 174 million gallons (800 million litres) of water with a dam height of seventy-nine feet (24 m). An osprey was sighted here in 1999.

20 *The Three Peaks*

Garsdale, Dentdale, Barbondale, Kingsdale, Ribblesdale — the Western Dales are unrivalled in their scenic beauty. J B Priestley considered them the finest countryside in Britain:

'...with their magnificent, clean and austere outlines of hill and moor, their charming villages and remote whitewashed farms, their astonishing variety of aspect and appeal, from the high gaunt rocks down to the twinkling rivers.'

William Hazlitt, in his *Visits to Remarkable Places* published in 1841, was not similarly impressed:

'It is a wild and, in many parts, a dreary region — a long ridge of hills covered with blackheath or bare stone. All round Ingleborough the whole country seems to have been so tossed, shaken and undermined by the violence which at some period broke it up.'

It is, of course a matter of opinion, but I cannot imagine any area in the county less 'dreary' than the Western Dales.

The most impressive landscape for me surrounds Ingleborough, a commanding upland height and the middle summit of the Three Peaks of Penyghent, Whernside and Ingleborough. Each summer, when our children were small, the family would spend a week in a friend's cottage at West Borran Head, near High Bentham, and walk for many happy miles along lonely footpaths.

This is a wild, beautiful landscape of spectacular waterfalls and rock-strewn gorges, cairns and caverns, enchanted glassy pools and bone-white limestone. It is breathtaking. It is the landscape of poetry:

'Mark these rounded slopes
With their surface fragrance of thyme and beneath
A secret system of caves and conduits; hear these springs
That spurt everywhere with a chuckle
Each filling a private pool for its fish and carving
Its own little ravine whose cliffs entertain
The butterfly and lizard; examine this region
Of short distances and definite places:
What could be more like a Mother or a fitter background
For her son, the flirtatious male who lounges
Against a rock in the sunlight ...'

(from *In Praise of Limestone* by W H Auden)

A cobbled street twists between sturdy
terraces in Dent Village. This is a
secluded, beautiful area of scattered
homesteads, sprawling grassy green
slopes, well-wooded valleys, dark crags
and soaring fells, described by the
writer and musician Mike Harding
as 'the bonniest of all the dales'.

I remember leaning over this bridge twenty or more years ago watching the fast-running waters of Clapham Beck with my children. We loved this beauty spot quietly hidden away in a narrow wooded valley below Ingleborough. A particular memory of this bridge was when my eldest son Richard, aged three, pulled off his shoe, which dropped off into the waters below and floated out of sight. Maybe this was a clever ruse, for I then had to carry him all the way back to West Borran Head near High Bentham, where we were staying.

Just over the border from Cumbria is the immense Ribblehead Viaduct, constructed in the 1870s by the Midland Railway Company for the passage of trains between Settle and Carlisle. An army of 2,000 workers descended on this wild moorland setting, living several sprawling shanty towns with names like Batty Green, Sebastopol and Jericho. The viaduct, over 100 feet (30 m) high and a quarter of a mile (400 m) long, spans the bog of Batty Moss and is built on a bed of concrete six feet (2 m) thick overlaid onto solid rock.

Right
The dark crags of naked rock and rock-strewn slopes rising above the tracts of treacherous marshes near Settle are called Attermire Scars. Formed 300 million years ago as sediments beneath a primeval sea, and later crushed and lifted by major earth movements, these rough-hewn hills look grim and silent beneath the lowering sky.

A dark and ominous sky spreads over the distinctive shape of Ingleborough. 'As on a pedestal stands the mass of Ingleborough', wrote the naturalist Reginald Farrer of nearby Ingleborough Hall in 1908, 'big, bold and flat-topped seen from afar.' This immense mass of carboniferous limestone, topped with a fifteen-acre (6 ha) plateau of Millstone Grit, is honeycombed with a network of natural shafts, caves, potholes and passages. It rises 2,373 feet (723 m) above sea level, and stands in majestic isolation from the other two mountains of the Three Peaks — Whernside (the highest of the three) and Penyghent.

Like one great crusted billow,
Ingleborough, shrouded in snow,
stands in all its austere winter beauty.
The tracks of some hardy walker can
be seen skirting the limestone
pavement in the foreground.

ACKNOWLEDGEMENTS

Photographs by

Dorothy Burrows, pages 17 bottom, 22, 27 top & bottom, 33 top, 37, 38 top, 42, 45, 52, 53, 54, 93, 133.

Chris Craggs, page 18 bottom.

John Critchley/English Heritage Photographic Library, page 20.

Alan Curtis, pages 58 bottom, 67 top & bottom, 72, 92 bottom.

Mike Kipling, pages 6, 60, 66, 68, 71, 77 top, 78 top & bottom, 79, 80-1, 81, 82, 84 top & bottom, 85 bottom, 86 top & bottom, 92 top, 98, 100, 112, 114, 116, 118 top & bottom, 126, 142.

John Morrison, pages 28, 31 top & bottom, 32, 33 bottom, 34, 36, 38 bottom, 39 left, 39 right, 40, 41, 46 top & bottom, 48, 50-1, 51, 55, 58 top, 59, 74, 85 top, 108 top & bottom, 109 bottom, 119, 120, 120-1.

Colin Raw, pages 8, 10, 12, 16, 18 top, 18-19 bottom, 30, 44, 47, 56, 61, 88, 90, 91, 94, 96, 97, 101, 102, 103, 106, 109 top, 110, 113, 115, 122, 123, 124, 128, 129 top, 130, 132, 134, 135, 136, 138, 141, 143.

Roger Redfern, pages 14, 17 top.

Bob Skingle/English Heritage Photographic Library, page 21.

David Tarn, pages 2, 62, 64, 65, 70-1, 72-3, 76, 77 bottom, 87, 104-5, 127, 129 bottom, 139, 140-1.

Jonty Wilde/Yorkshire Sculpture Park, pages 24, 25, 26.

The extract from the poem by Joan Ingilby on page 128 is reproduced by kind permission of Marie Hartley MBE.
The extract from *In Praise of Limestone* by W H Auden on page 137 is reproduced by kind permission of Faber & Faber.